It's Over

poems by

Susan Wolbarst

Finishing Line Press
Georgetown, Kentucky

FINISHING LINE PRESS

www.finishinglinepress.com

It's Over

For my son, Zachary Shpak, always an inspiration

ACKNOWLEDGMENTS

California Quarterly: "After" and "Badassery"
The Ledge Poetry and Fiction Magazine: "Seven Thousand Miles"
Naugatuck River Review: "Trust"
California State Poetry Society Poetry Letter: "Where's Ginny?'
Alchemy and Miracles, nature woven into words: "Watching the Perseids in Gualala,"
"Proximity," "At Grover Hot Springs" and "Have you seen the light?"
Pioneertownlit.com: "Polish Woman, 1943?"
Plainsongs: "Parking Lot Present"
Whisky Blot Journal: "Dos Cervezas in Merida, Mexico"
Poetry Now: "Diagnosis" and "In the Ladies Room"
Yolo Crow: "Last Fall Tomatoes"

Publisher: Leah Huete de Maines
Editor: Christen Kincaid
Cover Art: "A Meadow at Sunset" by Paul Huet circa 1845; in public domain,
Courtesy of National Gallery of Art, Washington.
Author Photo: Dave Shpak
Cover Design: Elizabeth Maines McCleavy

Order online: www.finishinglinepress.com
also available on amazon.com

Author inquiries and mail orders:
Finishing Line Press
PO Box 1626
Georgetown, Kentucky 40324
USA

Contents

It's Over

Sipping from my plastic tumbler of cheap red wine—
carried carefully from the tavern—
I notice she has stopped breathing.

The sudden absence of that noisy struggle
which has rattled her shoulders and chest for days
takes a second to absorb.

"Tom," I say to my brother, sitting nearby, reading,
"Look. It's over." It's Friday, the 13th of December,
at 7:26 p.m. I note the time on the wall clock,
the room so quiet I can hear the clock's hands move.

A ping on my cell phone at that exact second
will turn out to be a rejection from a magazine.

There's a "do not resuscitate" order, so, for the moment,
there's no urgency. My brother leaves to tell a nurse,
but they're all having dinner in the break room.
We decide not to bother them.

My mother lies in a pool of light, radiant,
white hair, thin as lace, capping her small head.
We kiss her face, still warm,
skin waxy and already golden.

We sit with her a while longer in the quiet,
aware of, but not hurrying to,
the long list of things we need to do next.

After

Fourteen people have survived suicidal jumps off the Golden Gate Bridge in the past 22 years. "Jump survivor Kevin Hines said he remembered landing in the water and that a creature kept him afloat. According to bystanders, it was a sea lion."
—San Francisco Chronicle

I didn't expect this.
The water is very cold and I am here.
I see sunshine and I am here.
I taste salt and I am here.
I hear the highway overhead
on the orange bridge, thrumming.
I can't turn my head to look.
I bob on the waves, remembering
the hard smack on the water. I will never
forget how hard it felt, how loud in my ears.
I expected that to be my last thought.
But I am here because of you.
I can't see you, but I know you're
under me because I feel warmth and
softness. You decided to keep me afloat
so I can breathe. I'm not sure why you did this.
I'm not sure I could keep upright by myself.
I'm not sure I can tell you how much I love you.
We have no shared language.
I love you more than I've ever loved anyone
or anything. I love everything here: the salt, the cold,
the sunshine, the thrumming, the bobbing.
But most especially, I love you.
I am telling you that over and over in my thoughts.
It all seems perfect to me now
because I am here. And you are here with me.
I hear a motor boat approaching
and feel its wake moving me.
I feel you dive away and cold
fills the space where you were.
Come back—I didn't thank you.
I didn't finish letting you know
how much I love you.
Someone from the boat
is yelling down to me, but
I don't understand. I can't listen.
Too much noise in my head.
I only know that I am here.
I only wish that I could
swim away with you.

Seven Thousand Miles

My son lives in a tent.
I pretend he's at summer camp.
I send him boxes of cookies.
When he Skypes me,
he's tan and handsome
and happy, aiding me in
my summer camp delusion.
People can enjoy
their time in the military.
He looks thin, so I
keep mailing cookies.
I think of him in his tent,
offering his buddies
some well-traveled
Girl Scout cookies
in a place no Girl Scout
has ever sold her wares.
I think of him chewing,
seven thousand miles away,
closing his eyes, leaning
his head back and smiling
at the homey
tastes of peanut butter
and chocolate.
I think of him laughing.
I think of him alive.

The Taste of Pleasure
(For Jake)

He could feel the chill as soon as he opened the door
and stepped onto the basement stairway.
With each step, it got cooler and closer to the hubbub.
All the cold things were there, arrayed temptingly on tables.

In the daylight pouring down from high-up windows, the boys
maneuvered deftly through the crowd among tables laden with cheese and
    fish,
bottled milk and cream, slabs of butter, crocks of pickles, kegs of beer.
Meat was at the opposite side of the expanse—as far from the dairy as
    possible.

Their mother trailed them, greeting neighbors and friendly vendors as she
    passed.
The boys rushed, then waited impatiently for her at their destination—a
    table with a blue cloth
and huge crockery bowls, each one covered with its own colorful cloth.
The boys were jumping up and down by the time she got there.

Their mother held up two fingers, smiling, and the farmer's wife grinned
back showing a gap where one of her teeth was missing.
She picked up a small bowl and ladled into it the thick sour cream
that formed a pillow for the red, black and dark blue berries she heaped on
    top.

She served the younger boy first, causing his older brother to bristle.
A long time later, it seemed to him, he got his own luxurious bowl.
He was pleased to see the farmer's wife had filled it higher than his brother's.
Eighty-five years later, he would remember the taste of pleasure.
He would describe it, smiling, to his children and grandchildren.

It was the first happy memory they'd heard of his childhood—
spent in a time and place remembered for unimaginable sorrow and terror.
Feeding him berries and sour cream—much inferior to the farmer's wife's
    product, I'm sure—
had accidentally conjured up a shining morning with an indulgent young
    mother
enjoying the pleasure of watching her boys eat their treats, unaware of the
    darkness to come.

Swinging

Four sisters sit, shoulders touching,
on the porch swing
print dresses clashing riotously.

Their many hours together in the hot kitchen
produced a meal blessed lengthily by their father.
Heaped on china plates,
it was praised by disappearing,
gravy trails erased by biscuits
before the juicy pie finale on the same plates.
Then the sisters cleaned up.

Their chattering finally done, like the dishes,
the quiet sisters rock the creaking porch swing,
their thoughts busy as cricket conversations
pulsing in the pastures all around them.
One wishes for a husband.
One who has a husband wishes for a baby.
The one who has a baby and a husband
wishes for homemade peach ice cream.
One wishes to go to New York City
and never come back.

The last is the first to get her wish,
surprising friends and family by leaving.
Sixty years later, she will surprise herself
by changing her mind and coming back,
drawn to sit again in a porch swing—
not this exact one, because her family's farm will be long gone—
but one quite like it, with that familiar creak,
in the very same town where she was born.
She will find it a comfort to be known and understood,
to grow old as part of something older than herself.

Now, two sisters dead, the other too busy,
she swings alone in sleepy twilight,
listening to descendants of the crickets
which once provided background
for the silent chorus of four sisters' longings.
These crickets seem to know the old songs perfectly,
exactly as she remembers them.

Trust

Folding her dead mother's dress
she barely felt it.

> Two sisters and an in-law
> filling brown paper sacks
> with mother's homemade dresses,
> worn almost transparent;
> their flowers, dots and plaids
> faded like old photos.
> (See here, on her quilt,
> the exact same fabric.)
> Partial to pink, mother also
> loved her aqua and her lilac.
> Mother made these dresses over years
> using one outdated pattern
> which still sits beside her Singer,
> creased and tissue-thin, full of pinholes.

Curious, she held it toward the light:
There! Matchbook-size, in the hem.

> Startled by the sound of ripping,
> the others turn to see her
> unfold a $5 bill,
> clean from many washings.
> Right away, the moment changes
> from sad and sorry duty to egg hunt,
> tearing mother's dresses,
> then her purses and her mattress,
> extracting 5s and 10s and 20s
> from the linings, hems and
> pockets—real and false—
> which came this close to staying hidden,
> moving right along in grocery sacks
> to the Goodwill dress rack, size large.

Slide Show

We watch her life pass
in chronologically random
color slides. Her gray
crewcut, growing in
after it all fell out.
Her curly red hair
of childhood.
She is holding her baby.
She is a grandmother.
She is a little girl.
She is pregnant.
She is a schoolteacher.
She is married
She is graduating from college.
She is baking pies,
her smile so big
it can barely be contained.
She is holding a lobster up
close to a child's face
so he can appreciate it
before it becomes dinner.
She is wearing Birkenstocks
in the snow. The slides
are hypnotic, but hard
to watch, knowing
she is gone. "A big hole,"
her husband says,
tapping his chest
gently with a fist.

Before Joanie

For everyone who worked there,
time was neatly divided into
two sections:
before Joanie and after Joanie.
Nobody added "was murdered"—
it was understood.

Before Joanie, people ate
their lunches outdoors on spring
days, enjoying the smell of fresh-cut
grass, the delicate pink buds opening.
Patients wandered around, savoring
fresh air as nurses ate sandwiches nearby.

Joanie had eaten what turned out
to be her last lunch on such
a perfect day, everything smelling of
grass and earth and flowers.
She was gathering up her lunch things
when someone killed her.
A witness ran to the guardhouse.

Alarms went off, guards appeared,
the entire place went on lockdown.
No one could go outdoors for months
as spring melted into broiling summer.
After Joanie, everything kept changing.
Fences went up, dividing the grounds.

Patients couldn't go outside in
groups, or without supervision.
Outdoor areas for staff were no longer
shared with patients. No one relaxed
for a second. All staff carried alarms.
Some never ate outdoors again.

Joanie had a long record at the hospital
and would have retired within a year or two.
A shy woman, she had planned to move closer to her
daughter to spend more time with grandchildren.
She would've been surprised to see how often
her name came up. She never planned
to become such a celebrity.

Last Night in the Blue Bed

I admit I've grown attached to this old iron bed
purchased years ago in Sacramento. Rescued
from leaning up against a guy's garage,

rusty and covered with spider webs.
My husband was skeptical, but I bought
it anyway, shelling out 25 bucks, which seemed

like a lot more then than it does now.
The seller helped my husband load the heavy pieces
into a borrowed truck and we took it home.

After sanding and priming, I painted it a cheerful color
I think of as Greek blue, often seen on Mykonos or Santorini,
framing bright white doorways as, I'm told, a good luck charm.

With a supportive mattress and some homemade quilts,
the blue bed served us well for many years (I hate to count
how many.) We have gotten our $25 worth.

We did not conceive our only child in the blue bed—
he was already born when we acquired it. What we did do was snuggle
and sweat, dream and nightmare, fight and make up.

Our last night in the blue bed drew me into a random recap
of all its locations, my brain racing through snapshots
of days and years, houses and moves, friends and neighbors

whose fates are unknown. Now the house is being sold
and we have no room for the blue bed. No one in the family wants it.
The bed is headed for the giant dumpster in the driveway,

a preview of unwanted endings to come.

How It Works

The cover of the book
had a pale pink border,
that shade associated
with baby girls, never
my favorite color.
Inside the border, a black
and white photo of fish swimming.
I don't remember the title.

"Read this," my father said,
"And if you have any questions,
ask me after." My mother sat
beside him, silently sipping
her cocktail. They seemed
smugly conspiratorial. What
weren't they telling me? Why?

I went to my room and read the book—
a thin volume filled mostly with
more black and white animal
photos. There was only one picture, at the end,
of a human: a woman nursing her baby.
Even that photo was somewhat
shocking then because it showed
an actual breast, an actual baby
sucking on it. I stared at it
for a long time, wondering where
breasts come from and if I would ever have any.

None of the words kids seem thankfully
familiar with now—penis, vagina,
that sort of thing—
made it into the pink book,
although it discussed fertilizing
eggs, as in how fish do it,
fertilize their eggs, that is.

Human reproduction didn't make it
into the text, any more than it made
it into the photos. When I finished,
I told my father I was done, and tried to

give the book back to him. "No, it's for
you," he said. "You may want to read it
again some time." I seriously doubted this.
"Do you have any questions?" I shook my head.

I didn't make the leap from animals to humans, so I was
confused by the book and why it was given. But I sensed
the book was a substitute for something; that somehow it
stood in for something too uncomfortable and embarrassing to discuss.
I retreated to my room, where I tossed the book under my bed,
never to be opened again. I knew
I'd need to seek my answers elsewhere.
I didn't know that many of the places I looked
would be as opaque and unhelpful
as that slender pink book.

Palm Sunday 1959

The significance of the palms meant nothing to me.
What was significant to me is that I would get to have a palm—
my own actual frond from a real palm tree. It did not come easily.

Palms were only being given to actual churchgoers, not
to child Sunday Schoolers. So that meant
I had to convince my mother to go to church with me.

My mother was not a churchgoer. She had her fill of churchy ways
as a Baptist child. She never entered a church unless for a wedding
or a funeral or some other socially pressured thing she
couldn't get out of. Palm Sunday was not such an event
and neither was Easter or Christmas, in her religious calendar
of entirely blank days. I begged her, telling her how much I wanted a
     palm frond
and she surprised me by capitulating and off we went, dressed up,
at least one of us happy. She wore a new hat. Why, of all days
and all available topics, did the pastor choose that day to preach about
     why women
should not work outside the home? It was almost like he aimed an
     arrow straight
at my mother's heart. She had worked at a paying job since the day my
     younger brother
started first grade. Even my greedy desire for a palm frond was
     overwhelmed
by feeling my mother's rage at the minister's words, ricocheting
off her, like the squiggly black lines showing anger in a comic strip.

I couldn't wait for the service to end, which it finally did. I was given
an actual palm frond to take home. It was as big as me. I had never seen
     one before.
I have no idea where they got the truckload of semi-dried-out palm
     fronds
distributed to the churchgoers, each frond trending away from its
     spirited green
youth toward a brownish-gray look of death by the time it was placed
in our hands. I was excited to touch it, quickly learning that the leaves
     had edges
sharp as knives. "Don't ever ask me to go with you to church again," my
     mother said,

unnecessarily, as we drove home. I raced inside and tacked the frond to
    my bedroom wall,
enjoying the scent of it. I imagined this as what the tropics smell like—
    dusky sweet rot.

I had never been to the tropics or seen a real palm tree, although I had a
    plastic one on a small
plastic island in my pet turtle's plastic dish. Connecticut in April smelled
    mostly like stale snow and mud and a kind of desperation. I found
    myself pointlessly kicking
rock-hard snowbanks anointed with yellow dog pee and crusted with
    black tar and pebbles.
I was totally sick of the cold, the red rubber boots, lost mittens and the
chapping wind which bit my face the minute I walked out the door.
    I was ready for some flowers, some grass,
some warmth. But now I could leave our yard's dirty snowbanks and sit
in my chilly bedroom admiring my dying palm frond, imagining that
    some day I might visit the hot humid place
it had lived. In the seemingly-endless New England winter, that was as
    close as I got to hope.

Vitamins and Supplements

Every morning, in a pretty pile
beside the breakfast plate
and steaming mugs of coffee are
our talismans, our horseshoes,
our rabbits' feet.
Some glisten like jewels,
others are much less flashy
tablets the color of sandstone
or sawdust. The turmeric stands out
bravely in bright orange.
The lutein is a warm dark red,
shaped like a tiny football.
None are white. I wonder if this
is the result of market research.
I've read many articles warning
that all of these are—at best, a useless
waste of lots of money—at worst, made
from toxic stuff and heavy metals
in countries offering consumers
nothing in the way of protection.
How ironic that we swallow them daily
for protection against heart disease,
the dreaded inflammation, the terrors of
cancer and macular degeneration. Each
day, the little pile offers hope
of keeping brain cells perky, hearts
sturdy, cells nourished with whatever
might be missing in the red wine
and the flank steak with eggplant
and tomato ragout, or the spinach salad,
or whatever else we happen to be enjoying.
Is whatever obscure thing is missing
from our diet found in the pretty piles?
We hope so, as it's part of our plan to stay
healthy and be active and not eat crap or
drink too many cocktails and fall
getting out of the hot tub or
fall asleep in a board of supervisors
meeting as it moves to its eleventh hour.
Will we know our own personal eleventh hour
when it comes? Or will it be just another inconvenient
surprise, like when Costco runs out of B-complex?

Cell Phones Are Drama Queens

Always carelessly getting lost,
falling out of pockets,
diving into toilets—
they'll do anything
to get attention.

Mine went through a complete
wash cycle recently
still in the back pocket
of my jeans, where
I like to carry it.

So it's in the washer
banging each time
it goes around
and the flashlight
is somehow turned on.

I learned that the washer
won't open mid-cycle
so I had to keep hearing
the banging and
watching the flashing

for what seemed like forever.
Then it was over. Amazingly,
the glass was only slightly chipped.
more amazingly, it
still worked.

The phone still let me access
my life—all my
contact information,
my calendar
my apps.

So I forgive it for being
a drama queen, for staying
in my pocket to ride through
a wash cycle just because.
That phone is a wonder.

Among the Leopard Sharks

My husband spots it first—a dark
slender shape in the water,

a shadow until sunlight catches
its golden leopardskin markings.

We stop paddling and peer into the water,
seeing them everywhere. Countless sharks

dart in and out of the eel grass,
some small, some five feet long.

Females are the biggest. Sinuous in the sandy shallows
they call home, lithe and supple, in constant motion,

sometimes rising close enough to the surface their black
dorsal fins slice through the water. They circle our kayak

as if hopeful of something, or merely curious.
Do they see us as food? I wonder.

I learn they exist only in one stripe of Pacific Coastal
waters between Oregon and Mazatlán, Mexico.

Not straying from their birthplaces, each group has
its own genetics. Tomales Bay leopard sharks differ

from those in La Jolla. Considered harmless to humans,
the only documented case of leopard sharks attacking

a person was in 1955, in Trinidad Bay, California. Scientists
surmise the cause was likely the diver's nosebleed.

Unlike leopard sharks' laissez-faire attitude
toward people, humans like to eat them,

endangering the sharks. The payback:
leopard sharks are loaded with mercury.

Louie's

It was called Rowayton News to the uninitiated, everyone else called it
  Louie's.

Before we go any further, I have to tell you I have no idea who Louie was.
The owner? The guy at the cash register? No idea. Once I set foot
in Louie's, I was focused on one thing only—commerce. The power
  of exchanging money for desirable goods.
There was a slight step up to get into the small shop, and when we
stepped inside, the wooden floors creaked. The place smelled of tobacco
and Bazooka bubble gum. Right inside were piles of newspapers—the
best seller being the impressively fat *New York Times Sunday Edition*,
stacked right on the counter, an easy grab for rushing customers, who
could leave their quarter on the counter. Other items near the front of the
store were packs of cigarettes, gum, cigars, magazines like *Time, Look* and
Life, Good Housekeeping and *Playboy*. None of this was a bit interesting
to my brother or me. We headed straight to the back of the store—the
dimly-lit repository for candy, D.C. and Marvel Comics, folding paper
kites and a freezer full of coveted root beer popsicles. Before we went into
the store, our father would give us a financial quiz: how many nickels
make a quarter? Or how many dimes make a dollar? Then he would give
us each a dime and turn us loose in our favorite store in town. In fairness,
the town was not exactly a shopping haven—it did have a hardware store
and a grocery store and that may have been it.

We cared mainly about what a dime would buy at Louie's: anything we
  wanted.

The choice, repeated every Sunday, on the newspaper pickup mission,
was agonizing. All the merchandise was so tempting, so glossy or sticky
and sweet. My brother—who couldn't read yet—usually went for a candy
bar or two, since they cost only a nickel. He struggled to decide between
Snickers, Milky Way, Hershey's, Butterfinger, Three Musketeers, Sky Bar,
Chunky and Charleston Chew. Sometimes he would be distracted from
candy long enough to buy a 5-cent pack of baseball cards, which came
with its own thin card-sized slab of bubble gum, traditionally stuffed into
a small mouth immediately after completing the purchase.

Learning to blow bubbles was important. And it took awhile to master
  that skill,
resulting in the usual gum sticking to the face (and for girls, the hair) in
  the interim.

I often bought a comic book—especially if the adventure featured a female protagonist like *Batwoman, Supergirl* or *Wonder Woman.* I also liked *Little Lulu* and *Little Dot.* Then there were *Archie* comics, which presented such a comforting vision of being a teenager. Hanging out at the soda shop every day after school to dance to the jukebox! It seemed like such a distant aspiration in the days of our excursions to Louie's. Our father—usually tremendously impatient—entertained himself reading the front page of his freshly-purchased paper, or chatting with the steady stream of acquaintances showing up on the same Sunday
morning errand,
while we browsed and deliberated with tremendous
seriousness about the most important decisions either of us
would make that week.

Memories

Like tiny Houdinis,
they are mummy-wrapped,
chained in chests
resting on the bottom of the sea.

I pretend they're gone for good
and I can live entirely in the present.

But I know they may show up at any time,
at the bottom of a martini glass,
in a foghorn,
coded inside the deepest dream, or
even in a quiet restaurant,
disconcertingly arrayed on a white
china tray
like tender asparagus
tempting a careless reach.

Wherever they're hiding,
they remain quietly alert,
sudden as switchblades,
poised.

Where's Ginny?

We always go to your favorite restaurant,
always order the same thing, as if adhering

to the routine will somehow make things revert
to how they used to be. We split a Reuben

sandwich and an order of sweet potato fries.
I order a glass of wine for each of us—you white,

me red—and we eat in the sunshine on the patio.
"We should take a boat trip down the Mississippi River,"

you say, not registering how impossible that would be.
That would be great, I say, but actually thinking

about you wandering around the boat all night
in fuzzy slippers, slipping and falling overboard.

Thinking about logistics of travel with you
in your current confusion gives me a headache.

Have you read any good books lately?
I ask, wondering if you can still

decode words on a page.
"I like this chardonnay," you say.

You eat three bites of your sandwich as I
wolf down my half and way too many fries.

You tear the rest into little pieces you intend
to feed your dog when you get home.

Eat your sandwich, Ginny. But you're already
packaging its pieces in your folded-up napkin,

stuffing it into your empty purse. You are skin
and bones. *Would you like some dessert? I noticed*

*they have banana bread. Do you remember making
it for our writers' group?* No answer. *Yours*

was the best I've ever eaten. Do you like peanut butter?
No answer. Would you like a peanut butter chocolate chip cookie?

But you're done thinking about food.
You smile, with a dreamy look passing

over your face that reminds me of the old you.
"A boat trip down the Mississippi River," you repeat.

Watching the Perseids in Gualala

(Note: Gualala is a small town (population: about 2,000) in Mendocino County, California. Its coastal location makes it prone to unpredictable fog any time of the day or night.)

Always in August, it seems to get going around midnight, or soon after.
One meteor dropping hard, like a bounced tennis ball, then,

before you can even make a wish,
another cascading down, dragging its tail like a confession.
Then another, in no particular rush, then another.

If the moon's not too bright, we may see
thirty, fifty or a hundred an hour—all over the sky—
so many, I feel a need to stretch out my eyes to see the whole show.

Then, with a militaristic efficiency
(so contrary to the wild painterly feast which preceded it),
a stealthy blanket of fog erases everything.
Sky gone, show over.

Polish Woman, 1943?

She runs, naked,
through an unnamed Polish town,
her hair and makeup
surprisingly intact, stylish.
Her face exemplifies terror.
She runs, naked.
Someone's life was risked
to take this photograph.
Life-sized, black and white,
hanging in London's Imperial War Museum.
I am rooted in front of it for a long time.
She runs, naked.
I can't move.
Which part of me
is most mesmerized?
The Polish part,
the Jewish part,
the female part,
the human part?
I'm guessing that shortly after
the shutter snapped,
she was killed—
naked, as she ran.
Unless, as cats will
sometimes do
with cornered prey,
they decided to
play with her first.

Parking Lot Present
(for Jane)

It's the season of wedging
holidays into crannies of working,
shopping through lunch and in darkness
for the annual torrent of tissue and ribbon.

Extra chairs borrowed for visiting family.
Huge meals gobbled dodging alligators—
layoffs, divorce, unfortunate stock deals—
which bite into conversation when we overdrink.

Which brings me to this moment.
My house overflowing with the people I love most,
I hide in my car, in the library parking lot.
My hands, raw from scouring, unfurl in warm pockets.
Others eye my parking space, but I'm not leaving.
This time to breathe alone is my gift, with love, to me.

Dos Cervezas in Merida, Mexico

Find a place to be at 4 p.m.
to experience the rain,
more predictable in July
than a Yucatecan clock.

I choose shelter under
an oversized green umbrella
at an outdoor café,
securing my table
and dos cervezas.
This lasts longer
than a one-beer rain.

Turning on like a faucet,
the jungle downpour
soaks summer cottons
to the skin in seconds.

Neither waiters nor iguanas
run through these water walls.
Surrounded by my
round water curtain,
I drink cold lagers named
Montejo and Negra Leon.
They pour down as easily
as the deluge.

In minutes, I feel
warm water flowing
over my sandaled feet
washing off the white dust
of Mayan ruins.

Finished,
just as I drain
my second bottle,
the miracle
repeats tomorrow,
right on time.

Diagnosis

There is a mysterious weightlessness
waiting for the diagnosis.

Big empty moments treading water,
over my head in the present tense
knowing that off in some lab, my chatty cells
tell my life's secrets to strangers.

I'm idly wondering if, someday,
this aimless hour will be remembered
as better than it seems right now,
because of what I don't yet know.

I also have to wonder
if my future, already, is compacting,
becoming small enough to fit inside an envelope,
small enough to fit inside a fortune cookie,
shrinking down to one line,
to one word,
breathe.

Have You Seen the Light?
(September 9, 2020)

The ocean, in its usual place,
is glowing, silver as the belly of a flopping
fish carried on its last ride in the talons of an osprey.

Nothing else is normal.

Everything is glowing orange,
an orange darkness starting about 11 a.m.
the color deepening as the hours slide by.
No sun. No clouds. No breeze. No birdsong.

Is this the way the sky looks right before the end of the world?
Is this the end of the world?

We look to the internet for answers.
Satellite time release photography shows massive waterfalls of smoke
gushing at us, over us, around us, all over this part of the world.

The air feels heavy, like it might start raining at any moment,
and I'm guessing every one of us peering into the orange
darkness is wishing it would rain enough
to extinguish the huge and terrifying fires feeding nearby.

But the internet forecast is clear—not a drop of rain in sight.
This light is truly scary, like our whole world is trapped
inside a jack o'lantern, impatiently waiting for Halloween to end.

Proximity

Recently, I got really close to a dead pelican—
close enough to see the ring of pale pink and yellow feathers around its
    eye.
I couldn't determine its cause of death. No obvious injury. Lying there,
as if merely stunned, it seemed ready to stretch out its wings any
    second
and hop off the cliff, to glide over fishing grounds, or swoop down
to sit, kinglike, among the smaller seagulls on the sand.

I've been close to dozens of jellyfish, mounded on the sand
like jellied desserts encased in cookie crumbs.
Once I saw nearly a thousand shipwrecked chitons, their bright orange
meat partly ripped from jointed white shells by sea birds.

Pebbles, kelp, and driftwood decorate this cemetery,
alive with clouds of tiny flies and the background percussion of waves.
One is close enough to feel eternity here.
Footprints mark the way.

At Grover Hot Springs
(Markleeville, CA)

Contentment comes in measured doses:
the breeze on a hot afternoon
the chance to read in a hammock
the 106-degree soak followed by
the sting of a quick rinse in a snow-melt cataract
the canned turkey chili heated on the camp stove
countless stars in the blackest sky
the vanilla scent of Jeffrey Pines
the campfire of logs so dry they snap
the cricket chorus extending into forever
the knowledge that even though
this isn't what life mostly is,
it's life that's there for the taking.

Badassery

My mother was a badass.
She wanted people to know that right away.
When she moved into the Veterans Home at age 88
she made sure everyone she met knew she wasn't
a Navy nurse or the surviving wife of some dead veteran.
She made sure they knew that she was a Marine—
one of the first class of women Marines
to graduate from boot camp at
Hunter College in New York—
a veteran of WW II.

She cemented her badass reputation at the Vets Home
by running off with a fellow vet one night.
I got the phone call from security about 2 a.m.
saying Mom and her friend had failed to return by curfew.
Security called the cops, who were out looking for them.
What do you know about this guy? Nothing, I said.

So an APB went out on my mother and her fellow vet.
The cops found them at a motel near a casino where they gambled
the night before on many things but not my mother's badass reputation.
"*Nothing is wrong*," my mother told me on the phone
after they'd been apprehended. "*We're fine. I don't see what the big deal is.
He just forgot where we were and how to get back, so we stayed at a motel.*"
Does he have Alzheimer's? "*Maybe, but he's a good driver*," she said.
The Vets Home took his keys away.

What they didn't take away was my mother's badassery.
There are many more men than women at the Vets Home,
so she got lots of attention, which she craved. One Halloween,
she wore a hot pink plastic hula skirt topped off by a bra
made of two fake coconut shell halves. She wore this contraption
over a turtleneck sweater, with red and yellow plastic leis
around her neck and gigantic wraparound sunglasses designed
to protect whatever remained of her vision. She sent pictures of herself
in this getup to my brother and me, to impress on us how hot she was
     at age 90.
The huge grin on her face in the photo said it all:
badass, loving every minute.

Last Fall Tomatoes

I hesitate to pick
these final ripe tomatoes
as if leaving them
attached, beckoning,
hangs onto summer
one more day.

Daylight savings and
Halloween have passed
yet a few tomatoes soldier on,
so full of sweetness
their tops crack into
star-shaped scars.

From the kitchen window
their sunburned cheeks
continually remind me
that their days are numbered
and tonight
they'll surely freeze.

But harvest means admitting
the annual inevitable:
another summer gone.
It's time for mud and heating bills,
winter greens, root vegetables,
dark days without tomatoes.

In the Ladies Room

Faucet water splashing
almost drowns her sounds
of sobs poured down the sink.

Others do their best to ignore her,
rushing through their urgencies
inside an O'Hare Airport Ladies Room.
They veer to dodge her,
then secretly appraise her
as they soap and rinse,
crumple paper towels,
primp, embellish, and
wheel their bags out the door
moving briskly from, or maybe to,
distant places visited
for important reasons.

She's the only one going nowhere,
ignoring intercom voices
droning flights, gates, times.
I'm pulled into her grief,
as familiar to me as a threadbare quilt.
I have also tried to wash pain
down drains of Ladies Rooms
away from public view
when there was nowhere else
and nothing else was possible.
Feeling the need to comfort,
I step behind her,
touch her shoulder,
can't keep from asking
if there's something I can do.
She unfolds upward,
face red in the mirror,
reflected mouth saying
soundlessly
my boy is dead.
My reflection tells hers
I'm so sorry
regretting the smallness
of my whispered words.

I watch her mirrored lips ask me
to tell her husband she's OK
then she bends again
toward the water
and the washing
and her pain.

I hurry out
to deliver her message,
relieved to have a purpose.
He waits outside the Ladies Room
quiet as a snowman,
a dry, pale version of his wife.
I recognize him right away
by the pieces that are missing.

Memoir

She liked the word "memoir,"
the way it filled her mouth, the way
it seemed to ring with possibilities.
She pictured a slow unraveling
of yarns. She pictured her violent past
threaded through a bucolic masquerade
of civility, the way a defense witness
can be tricked out in a soft white dress
to convince the jury she's truthful.

The few pieces of her memoir she's completed
are painfully truthful. To those who can't allow
themselves to believe her stories,
she offers the decomposing
newspaper clippings loosely stuffed
into scrapbooks with black pages.
"Here is the time my mother was arrested
for shooting at my father. See how
beautiful she looks in her picture."

What she looks in her picture is terribly confused,
as if she has lost her keys, or maybe found them,
but can't quite remember what they might unlock.
She looks like a person who has forgotten something
her children are counting on her to remember. Are
they still waiting to be picked up after ballet lessons?

Her aim was poor and her husband unscathed.
She was jailed only briefly,
before posting bail, then the police
quietly returned her to the crime scene—
her home of elegant order and style—
after removing all the guns.

There is elegant order and style to her daughter's memoir,
consisting, as it does, almost entirely of blank pages.
After delaying this project so long, the writer has become
terribly confused, having lost her keys, wallet and phone.
The computer is broken, she says. She can't answer
my emails because the email is broken.
She keeps a dear beagle. He is warm
if not helpful. She rests her socked feet lightly
on his sleeping back as she reads and re-reads
a dog-eared book describing how to write a memoir.

What Murderers Look Like

The first murderer I encountered
was a slight, bald man who
might have been an accountant,
except for his heavy gold jewelry
studded with huge chunks of turquoise.
At trial he described his profession as retired.
His crime was killing the handsome lover
of his trophy wife. *"I noticed him wearing my belt.*
Right then I knew. After he went down,
I took my belt back. I considered shooting
my wife, too, but she was begging me not to,
her makeup running, saying she loved me."
The second murderer was a pale 16-year-old boy
with a Beatle haircut. He never took the stand
and never said a word in court, aside from
confirming his name. He strangled a real estate
broker while she attempted to sell
his family home. She was cutting up fruit
in preparation for hosting an open house
when he attacked her. No one could say why
except the boy who wasn't talking.
He put her body in the bathroom and locked
the door, exiting through the window.
He used her car to take friends joyriding
while real estate agents toured the home.
They knocked on the bathroom door.
When no one answered, they assumed
it was occupied. It was—by someone my age,
a total stranger to the boy who strangled her.
The third was a woman who killed her
six-year-old daughter. She pleaded not guilty
by reason of insanity. She looked tired,
like any stressed-out mother
who can't remember what it's like
to sleep all night or do any private thing
without interruption.

At each of their trials,
I would look up from my notes
to study their faces for some indication
of … what? I thought I would
detect something unusual about them
or the others whose trials I watched later.
But I found nothing. Each murderer
looked exactly like you or me.

Susan Wolbarst lives and writes in Gualala, CA, a rural village of about 2,000 people in southern Mendocino County, CA. She can see the Pacific Ocean from her bedroom and sometimes—when weather conditions are right—she can hear seals barking. She writes narrative poetry and works part-time as a reporter for the local weekly newspaper, the Independent Coast Observer. The climate is temperate and the home she shares with her husband, Dave Shpak, is surrounded by redwoods. She previously lived in hot, dry Davis for over 20 years, craving a perch near the ocean the entire time.

In August of 2023, she won second place in the annual California State Poetry Society contest for a poem called "Badassery." In August of 2022, she won second place in the same contest for a poem named "After." She also won "honorary mention" in the same contest for a poem called "Where's Ginny?" about a close friend with Alzheimer's Disease. All of these poems are included in this book.

In April 2022, Susan created a yearly "Poetry for Everyone" event with the Gualala Arts Center. She continues to organize the event each April in honor of National Poetry Month. Participants are asked to read a favorite poem or two, written by themselves or anyone else. The first year, one attendee was a tourist who saw a flyer advertising the event in the local post office and wrote her first poem, which she brought to share. The group consensus was that it was darned good. Another year, a high school student courageously shared an honest and personal poem about breaking up with his girlfriend. "We've had people reading poems hundreds years old and those reading poems they wrote yesterday. It's always a surprise to see what people will bring to share," she said.

Susan's writing has been published in *Plainsongs, thewildword.com, pioneertownlit.com, The Whisky Blot, The Ledge Poetry and Fiction Magazine, Naugatuck River Review,* and others. Her poems have been anthologized in *Spirit of Place, Mendocino County Women Poets Anthology,* edited by Devreaux Baker et al. (2025) and *Alchemy and Miracles,* nature woven into words, edited by Cassandra Arnold (2023).

She self-published one cookbook in 1992. She loves messing around in kayaks, and travel, especially to countries beginning with "I" such as India, Italy and Israel. Susan also loves reading and cooking recipes from around the world in her three cast iron pans. She earned an MA in art from California State University, Sacramento and a BFA from the San Francisco Art Institute. Susan also attended Bennington College in Vermont.

www.ingramcontent.com/pod-product-compliance
Lightning Source LLC
Chambersburg PA
CBHW020220090426
42734CB00008B/1152